A Note From Rick Renner

I am on a personal quest to see a "revival of the Bible" so people can establish their lives on a firm foundation that will stand strong and endure the test as end-time storm winds begin to intensify.

In order to experience a revival of the Bible in your personal life, it is important to take time each day to read, receive, and apply its truths to your life. James tells us that if we will continue in the perfect law of liberty — refusing to be forgetful hearers, but determined to be doers — we will be blessed in our ways. As you watch or listen to the programs in this series and work through this corresponding study guide, I trust you will search the Scriptures and allow the Holy Spirit to help you hear something new from God's Word that applies specifically to your life. I encourage you to be a doer of the Word He reveals to you. Whatever the cost, I assure you — it will be worth it.

> Thy words were found, and I did eat them;
> and thy word was unto me the joy and rejoicing of mine heart:
> for I am called by thy name, O Lord God of hosts.
> — Jeremiah 15:16

Your brother and friend in Jesus Christ,

Rick Renner

Rick Renner

Never Forget

Copyright © 2021 by Rick Renner
P.O. Box 702040
Tulsa, OK 74170

Published by Rick Renner Ministries
www.renner.org

ISBN 13: 978-1-68031-992-7

eBook ISBN 13: 978-1-68031-993-4

How To Use This Study Guide

This five-lesson study guide corresponds to *"Never Forget" With Rick Renner* (Renner TV). Each lesson in this study guide covers a topic that is addressed during the program series, with questions and references supplied to draw you deeper into your own private study of the Scriptures on this subject.

To derive the most benefit from this study guide, consider the following:

First, watch or listen to the program prior to working through the corresponding lesson in this guide. (Programs can also be viewed at **renner.org** by clicking on the Media/Archive links.)

Second, take the time to look up the scriptures included in each lesson. Prayerfully consider their application to your own life.

Third, use a journal or notebook to make note of your answers to each lesson's Study Questions and Practical Application challenges.

Fourth, invest specific time in prayer and in the Word of God to consult with the Holy Spirit. Write down the scriptures or insights He reveals to you.

Finally, take action! Whatever the Lord tells you to do according to His Word, do it.

For added insights on this subject, it is recommended that you obtain Rick Renner's book *Unlikely — Our Faith-Filled Journey to the Ends of the Earth.* You may also select from Rick's other available resources by placing your order at **renner.org** or by calling 1-800-742-5593.

TOPIC

Never Forget To Remember God's Goodness to You

SCRIPTURES

1. **Psalm 103:2** — Bless the Lord, O my soul, and forget not all his benefits.

2. **2 Timothy 1:3** — I thank God, whom I serve from my forefathers with pure conscience, that without ceasing I have remembrance of thee in my prayers night and day.

3. **2 Timothy 1:4** — Greatly desiring to see thee, being mindful of thy tears, that I may be filled with joy.

4. **2 Timothy 1:5** — When I call to remembrance the unfeigned faith that is in thee, which dwelt first in thy grandmother Lois, and thy mother Eunice; and I am persuaded that in thee also.

5. **2 Timothy 1:6** — Wherefore I put thee in remembrance that thou stir up the gift of God, which is in thee by the putting on of my hands.

6. **2 Timothy 1:7** — For God hath not given us the spirit of fear; but of power, and of love, and of a sound mind.

7. **2 Timothy 1:8** — Be not thou therefore ashamed of the testimony of our Lord, nor of me his prisoner: but be thou partaker of the afflictions of the gospel according to the power of God.

GREEK WORDS

1. "without ceasing" — ἀδιάλειπτος (*adialeiptos*): without interruption, without an interval, without taking a break, or continuously; always or persistently

2. "remembrance" — μνεία (*mneia*): signified a statue, monument, or some type of memorial intended to be permanent; to memorialize

3. "of" — περί (*peri*): surrounding; encircling; about

4. "prayers" — δέησις (*deisis*): its various forms are translated prayer and petition more than 40 times in the New Testament; a request for a

concrete, specific need, usually some type of physical or material need, to be met; a petition

5. "greatly desiring" — ἐπιποθέω (*epipotheo*): intense desire; a craving, a hunger, an ache, a yearning, or hankering for something, a longing or pining for something; to strain after, to greatly desire; to have strong affection: a fervent passion

6. "tears" — δάκρυον (*dakruon*): a tear drop; plural, tears

7. "call to remembrance" — ὑπόμνησις (*hupomnesis*): to actively bring to memory; to keep a memory by me

8. "unfeigned" — ἀνυπόκριτος (*anupokritos*): authentic; genuine compared to what is pretended, simulated, faked, feigned, or phony; one who is authentic, sincere, or trustworthy; not hypocritical

9. "dwelt" — ἐνοικέω (*enoikeo*): to dwell in a house; to take up residency; to settle into a home; to be at home; to be a permanent indweller

10. "persuaded" — πείθω (*peitho*): convinced to the core; rock-solid certainty

11. "I put thee in remembrance" — ἀναμιμνήσκω (*anamimnesko*): a compound that means to repeat, to remember, to remind, to regather, or to recollect memories

12. "stir up" — ἀναζωπυρέω (*anadzoopureo*): compound of ἀνά (*ana*), ζῷον (*zoon*), and πῦρ (*pur*); the word ἀνά (*ana*) carries the idea of repeating an earlier action or doing something again; the word ζῷον (*zoon*) is from a word meaning to be enthusiastic, to be fervent, to be passionate, to be vigorous, to be wholehearted, or to be zealous; the word πῦρ (*pur*); is the Greek word for fire; compounded, to enthusiastically, fervently, passionately, vigorously, or zealously rekindle a fire until it burns brightly again; to stir a flame again; to stoke and rekindle the embers of a fire until it is once again burning brightly

13. "gift" — χάρισμα (*charisma*): derived from χάρις (*charis*), the word for grace; when it becomes charisma, it depicts something that is given or imparted by grace; historically, this word was used to describe that moment when the gods graced or donated supernatural ability, favor, or power to an individual; thus, this word meant a gracious gift; a person who has received a charisma has received a donation or an enablement from God that equips him in some supernatural manner

14. "spirit" — πνεῦμα (*pneuma*): spirit

15. "fear" — **δειλός** (*deilos*): a gripping fear or dread that produces a shrinking back or cowardice; a dread that saps one's ability to look at a problem head-on and causes him to retreat; to be timid or cowardice

16. "power" — **δύναμις** (*dunamis*): power; the idea of explosive, superhuman power that comes with enormous energy and produces phenomenal, extraordinary, and unparalleled results

17. "love" — **ἀγαπη** (*agape*): God's kind of love; high-level love; describes the admiration one had for a person or object; the onlooker was so taken by the object that he couldn't simply look at it, he gazed upon it and became affected by it even experiencing a loss of words to express the admiration and love for a person or object; high-level love; God's kind of love

18. "sound mind" — **σωφρονέω** (*sophroneo*): to be of sound mind; to be reasonable; to be balanced and levelheaded in the way one thinks; to think rationally

19. "according to" — **κατά** (*kata*): according to; being dominated by

20. "power" — **δύναμις** (*dunamis*): power; the idea of explosive, superhuman power that comes with enormous energy and produces phenomenal, extraordinary, and unparalleled results; the word depicts "mighty deeds" that are impressive, incomparable, and beyond human ability to perform; denotes miraculous power or miraculous manifestations

SYNOPSIS

The five lessons in this study on *Never Forget* will focus on the following topics:

- Never Forget To Remember God's Goodness to You
- Never Forget God's Goodness to Your Life
- Never Forget God's Promises
- Never Forget To Build Markers To Recall What God Has Done
- Never Forget People God Has Used To Be a Blessing to You

The emphasis of this lesson:

God has given you a special weapon to keep you in faith, and it is the power of *remembering*. You can either choose to remember the bad things that happened to you, or purposely remember God's goodness to

you. Let your memory work positively for you and realize there are some things you should never forget — particularly the goodness of God!

Located across the Neva River in Saint Petersburg, Russia, is the Russian Winter Palace, which was the residence of the Russian royal family during the winters. Inside the Winter Palace is a magnificent room called The Concert Hall, and it contains something very important for Russia: the tomb of Alexander Nevsky — the greatest soldier in the history of Russia.

In 1240, the Teutonic Knights began to move up through Europe into Scandinavia. From Scandinavia, they launched their attack against Russia, but Alexander Nevsky stopped them and drove them back. This etched a place for him in Russian history which was so notable that in 1740, Elizabeth, the daughter of Peter the Great — who was known as Empress Elizaveta — decided she would have a special casket made for his relics. It weighed one and a half tons, and it was fabricated of solid, pure silver.

In 1922, after the Bolshevik Revolution, it was moved to The Concert Hall of the Winter Palace. All of these years people have been coming to see the shrine of Alexander Nevsky. It's surrounded by 32 majestic columns that line The Concert Hall. The columns look like towering soldiers saluting the remains of Alexander Nevsky. History records the reason his body was placed there is to assure Russia *never forgets* the deeds of this notable soldier. Likewise, there are some things *we* should never forget! We need to remind ourselves of the great things God has done in our past.

Never Forget the Goodness of God

Sometimes you have to speak to your soul and tell it what to remember. During a low moment, David was tempted to forget all the good things God had done for him. He was worried about his future, and knew he needed to get a grip on himself. So he spoke to his soul and said, "Bless the Lord, O my soul, and forget not all his benefits" (Psalm 103:2).

My friend, if you're worried about your future, it may just mean you have a faulty memory because if you look at your past, you've been through things that are even more difficult than what you're facing right now. You walked through them successfully, and you're going to walk through the present difficulty victoriously as well!

When the apostle Paul was in prison in Rome suffering for his faith, he received a letter from Timothy who was in Ephesus. At the time the letter was written, Timothy was free, but facing a lot of problems in his church because of the raging persecution that had been unleashed by the emperor Nero.

The people Timothy thought he could always depend upon walked out on him and left his church. He felt abandoned, hurt, and he didn't know how he would face his future. So he wrote a letter to Paul who was in prison — the free man wrote to the imprisoned man to ask for help. Paul received Timothy's letter and started to answer him by saying, "I thank God, whom I serve from my forefathers with pure conscience, that *without ceasing* I have remembrance of thee in my prayers night and day" (2 Timothy 1:3). The words "without ceasing" — the Greek word *adialeiptos* — means *without interruption, without an interval, without taking a break, or continuously;* it means *always or persistently.*

In the program Rick shared, "I remember when my grandmother Renner was getting older. One day she said to me, 'Oh Ricky, I'm of no value to anybody; all I can do is sit here in this chair and pray for you.' I said, 'Grandma! What do you mean you're of no value? That may be the most powerful thing you can do — to sit in that chair and to pray for me, and to pray for others!'"

Paul was in prison; he couldn't see or fellowship with anyone, so he took advantage of the moment. And that's what you have to do in life! Maximize whatever place you are in. Paul basically said, "I'm in this place; I've got time on my hands, so I'm going to pray *without interruption, without an interval, without taking a break, continuously, always,* and *persistently.*"

You Have To Make a Decision To Remember Some Things

Paul said, "…I have remembrance of thee in my prayers night and day" (2 Timothy 1:3).

The word "remembrance" — the Greek word *mneia* — signifies *a statue, monument,* or *some type of memorial intended to be permanent.* It means *to memorialize an event or person.* When you see a statue of a person, what is the purpose of the statue? It's intended to remind you of that person and what they did in history — so you will *never forget.* In essence Paul said,

"Timothy, night and day in my prayers I'm erecting statues or monuments of you in the very presence of God, so everywhere God looks He sees you."

Paul wrote, "…I have remembrance of thee…" (2 Timothy 1:3). Even the word "of" is important because it is the Greek word *peri*, which means everything *surrounding* you; all that's *encircling* you; and everything *about* you. Paul was communicating, "I'm making concrete petitions to God on your behalf. I'm stacking the throne room of heaven with images of you, so every time God looks somewhere, He sees an image of you."

The apostle Paul said, "…I have remembrance of thee in my prayers…" (2 Timothy 1:3). The word "prayers" is the Greek word *deisis*, and its various forms are translated "prayer" and "petition" more than 40 times in the New Testament. It means *a request for a concrete, specific need, usually some type of physical or material need, to be met*. It denotes *a petition*.

In the program Rick shared, "I'm so thankful for people who pray for me. When you call out my name to God, you build an image of me in the presence of God." Likewise, when someone prays for *you*, they're building an image of *you* in the presence of God, so He sees you and is confronted with you. And when *you* pray for someone else, you're stacking heaven with *their* image, so God is confronted with *them*.

Paul continued, "Greatly desiring to see thee, being mindful of thy tears, that I may be filled with joy" (2 Timothy 1:4). "Greatly desiring" in Greek is the word *epipotheo*, and denotes *intense desire; a craving, a hunger, an ache, a yearning*, or *a hankering for something*. It pictures *a longing or pining for something*; it means *to strain after, to greatly desire*; and *to have strong affection*. It describes someone doubled over, yearning for something.

The Power of Your Memory

Paul yearned to see Timothy because he was aware of the turmoil and persecution taking place at that time, and acknowledged, "…being mindful of thy tears…" (2 Timothy 1:4). The word for "tears" in Greek — *dakruon* — is plural and means *tear drops*, and many of them. Some scholars say that when Paul received Timothy's letter he could see his tears on the letter.

And Paul, like a father in the faith, spoke to his young son by saying, "I'm aware of your tears, and I'm aware of what you're going through." And here we have *the power of memory*. Paul began to remind Timothy of something very important. Paul admonished, "When I call to remembrance the unfeigned faith that is in thee, which dwelt first in thy grandmother Lois, and thy mother Eunice; and I am persuaded that in thee also" (2 Timothy 1:5).

You have to intentionally call some things to remembrance — they don't come to you automatically. Paul said, "I'm going to call to remembrance a few things..." and started with "unfeigned" faith. What does "unfeigned" mean? The word *feigned* describes a hypocrite, someone insincere, and not real.

A hypocrite is someone who wears a mask and acts like something that he is not; he is "feigned" or inauthentic. That's why Jesus called the scribes and Pharisees hypocrites. It was the equivalent of saying, "You are nothing but a bunch of actors performing on a stage in front of people. You are hypocrites who just wear a mask, and don't mean one thing you're saying."

Do You Have a Real, Living Faith in God?

But Paul said Timothy's faith was "unfeigned" — the Greek word *anupokritos* — which means his faith was *authentic, genuine compared to what is pretended, simulated, faked, feigned, or phony*. It describes one who is *authentic, sincere, or trustworthy*, and *not hypocritical*. Paul was saying, "Timothy, you have a real, living faith which dwelt first in thy grandmother Lois, and thy mother Eunice; and I am persuaded that in thee also."

The word "dwelt" is the Greek word *enoikeo*, which means *to dwell in a house*; *to take up residency*; *to settle into a home*; *to be at home*; and *to be a permanent indweller*. It pictures one taking up residence in a house. Paul was saying, "Faith is so real in your grandmother and your mother, that it literally *lives* in them. It *thrives* in them. And Timothy, I'm convinced to the core that this same kind of faith is living and it's thriving inside *you!*"

"Wherefore I put thee in remembrance that thou stir up the gift of God, which is in thee by the putting on of my hands" (2 Timothy 1:6). The phrase "I put thee in remembrance," is a translation of the Greek word *anamimnesko*, a compound that means *to repeat, to remember, to remind, to regather*, or *to recollect memories*. Paul is saying, "I'm reminding you of these things, and I'm helping you recollect the right memories, that by remembering them you might stir up the gift of God that is in you."

Just like you use a poker to stir the embers in a flame, memory is a divine tool God has given to you. You have to make a choice: You can let your embers die down, or you can use the power of memory and stir up the gift of God that is in you.

Take Action! Before the Embers Burn Out — Reach Within Yourself and Rekindle the Fire in Your Heart

Rather than worry about a current financial dilemma, put it on pause and remember how God delivered you in a previous financial challenge. Rather than worry about a current relational conflict, put it on pause and choose to remember how God walked you through every previous relational disruption. You have to *choose* what you remember.

In the program Rick shared, "I can testify from my own life that in moments when I'm feeling a little low, I put everything on pause and intentionally remember all the valleys we've walked through — how God walked us out of low places into high places. And by the time I'm finished remembering, I'm no longer in a low place. My faith has been stirred up."

That is the power of memory. You have to intentionally let your memory work positively for you. If you don't make that choice, it will work negatively against you. You've got to make a decision to stir up the right memories and remember all the goodness of the Lord from your past.

Paul literally said, "I put thee in remembrance that thou stir up the gift of God, which is in thee by the putting on of my hands" (2 Timothy 1:6). "Stir up" — the Greek word *anadzoopureo* — is a compound of three Greek words — *ana*, *zoon*, and *pur*. The word *ana* carries the idea of *repeating an earlier action or doing something again*. The word *zoon* is from a word meaning *to be enthusiastic, to be fervent, to be passionate, to be vigorous, to be wholehearted*, or *to be zealous*. And the word *pur* is the Greek word for *fire*. When you compound these words, it means *to enthusiastically, fervently, passionately, vigorously, or zealously rekindle a fire until it burns brightly again; to stir a flame again; to stoke and rekindle the embers of a fire until it is once again burning brightly*.

Timothy's fire was on a low burn. He had to do something to stir it up again, so Paul said, "Timothy, remember!" Remember how God has been faithful to you in your past so you'll understand He's going to be faithful to you right now! Remember everything you've been through. Walk yourself from your past to your present in your memory, and by the time you get to your present moment, your heart will be burning brightly again. Remind yourself of all of these things, that by remembering them you might stir up the gift of God that is in you.

Power, Love, and a Sound Mind

In Second Timothy 1:7 Paul continued, "For God hath not given us the spirit of fear; but of power, and of love, and of a sound mind." The word "spirit" in Greek is the word *pneuma* and means just that — *a spirit*. My friend, when a *spirit* of fear enters the scene, it brings panic and worry. It throws you into a state of bewilderment, and you don't know what to do.

The word "fear" is the Greek word *deilos*, which describes *a gripping fear or dread that produces a shrinking back or cowardice*; it is *a dread that saps one's ability to look at a problem head on and causes him to retreat*. It can be translated *timid* or *cowardice*. A *spirit* of fear will cause you to want to hide rather than confronting what you need to confront.

"For God hath not given us the spirit of fear; but of power, and of love, and of a sound mind" (2 Timothy 1:7). The word "power" is a form of the Greek word *dunamis*, and it describes *power*. It carries the idea of *explosive, superhuman power that comes with enormous energy and produces phenomenal, extraordinary, and unparalleled results*. What is in you by the Holy Ghost is the full might of an advancing army. You've got an army on the inside of you that can move forward and drive back that spirit of fear. He has given you a spirit of love, meaning you can move in a spirit of love even if you're tempted to be afraid of people. God has given you power, love, and a sound mind.

"Sound mind" is the Greek word *sophroneo*, which means *to be of sound mind; to be reasonable; to be balanced and levelheaded in the way one thinks*; and *to think rationally*. When you have a spirit of fear, you don't think rationally; you worry about everything. You even imagine things are going to happen to you that will never happen because you're functioning in a *spirit* of fear — an irrational spirit.

Timothy was experiencing an irrational spirit of fear — he was worried. Paul wrote to him and said, "Timothy, what's wrong with you is you're just not remembering things well. Think of all that God has done for you and your family. If you look at your past, God's record with you is full of His goodness. He has always been faithful, and He's going to be faithful now. I remind you of this so that by remembering it, you will stir up the gift of God that is in you."

Forget Not All His Benefits!

My friend, you need to never forget what God has done for you, and that's why Psalm 103:2 says, "Bless the Lord, O my soul, and forget not all his benefits." You have to *speak* to your soul and *forget not* all His benefits. Choose what you remember, and by remembering the right things you will stir up the gift of God that is in you and put to flight any spirit of fear that is trying to operate in your life.

STUDY QUESTIONS

Study to shew thyself approved unto God, a workman that needeth not to be ashamed, rightly dividing the word of truth.
— 2 Timothy 2:15

1. Do you have a "benefit package" at your place of employment? What do you need to do to take advantage of the benefits? Likewise, you are promised a host of benefits in God's Word. What do you need to do to embrace and enjoy all the benefits from God's Word in your life? (*Consider* Joshua 1:8; Psalm 1:1-3; James 1:22; and Romans 10:17.)

2. God was faithful to you in the past — and He has not changed! You made it through all that you've already walked through, and you're going to continue to make it through victoriously both in the present and the future! (*See* Hebrews 13:8; and James 1:17.)

3. Take a moment to examine your heart. Have you yielded to a spirit of fear about something? *Resist* fear, and in its place *embrace* the promises of God.

   - **Healing**: Isaiah 53:4 and 5; 1 Peter 2:24; James 5:16; and Romans 8:11

   - **Protection**: Psalm 91:1-16; Psalm 103:4; Proverbs 1:33; and Proverbs 30:5

   - **Victory**: 1 Corinthians 15:57; Revelation 12:11; and 1 John 4:4

   - **Provision**: Philippians 4:19; 3 John 2; 2 Corinthians 8:9; Psalm 35:27; Psalm 115:14-16; and Psalm 23:1

- **God's wonderful plan for your life**: Jeremiah 29:11-13; Colossians 1:9-14; Colossians 4:12; Hebrews 12:1,2; Revelation 3:7,8; and Colossians 4:17

PRACTICAL APPLICATION

But be ye doers of the word, and not hearers only,
deceiving your own selves.
— James 1:22

1. Are you so physically and emotionally exhausted from dealing with an onslaught of problems that your spiritual fire is beginning to wane? Timothy was in that situation, and Paul admonished him to take action and stir up the gift of God inside him. Just as a person stokes coals in a fireplace, Timothy was to stir the waning embers in his heart. Take a moment to look and honestly observe the condition of *your* inward fire. Now proactively stir up the gift of God within you so it once again becomes ablaze!

2. Psalm 103:1,2 says, "Bless the Lord, O my soul: and all that is within me, bless his holy name. Bless the Lord, O my soul, and forget not all his benefits." To help you remember the Lord's benefits, write out an example of how each of the following has occurred in your life. Expect the Lord to continue to bless your present and future with even more examples of these benefits!

    - Forgiven from iniquities

    - Healed

    - Redeemed from destruction

    - Crowned with favor

    - Satisfied with good things

    - Blessed with renewed youth

    - Vindicated (cleared of blame or suspicion; declared innocent)

TOPIC

Never Forget God's Goodness to Your Life

SCRIPTURES

1. **Psalm 111:4** — He hath made his wonderful works to be remembered....

2. **2 Timothy 1:5** — When I call to remembrance the unfeigned faith that is in thee, which dwelt first in thy grandmother Lois, and thy mother Eunice; and I am persuaded that in thee also.

3. **2 Timothy 1:6** — Wherefore I put thee in remembrance that thou stir up the gift of God, which is in thee by the putting on of my hands.

4. **2 Timothy 1:7** — For God hath not given us the spirit of fear; but of power, and of love, and of a sound mind.

5. **Hebrews 10:32** — But call to remembrance the former days, in which, after ye were illuminated, ye endured a great fight of afflictions.

6. **Hebrews 10:33** — Partly, whilst ye were made a gazingstock both by reproaches and afflictions; and partly, whilst ye became companions of them that were so used.

7. **2 Corinthians 4:17** — For our light affliction, which is but for a moment....

GREEK WORDS

1. "persuaded" — πείθω (*peitho*): convinced to the core; rock-solid certainty

2. "I put thee in remembrance" — ἀναμιμνήσκω (*anamimnesko*): a compound that means to repeat, to remember, to remind, to regather, or to recollect memories

3. "stir up" — ἀναζωπυρέω (*anadzoopureo*): compound of ἀνά (*ana*), ζῷον (*zoon*), and πῦρ (*pur*); the word ἀνά (*ana*) carries the idea of repeating an earlier action or doing something again; the word ζῷον (*zoon*) is from a word meaning to be enthusiastic, to be fervent, to be

passionate, to be vigorous, to be wholehearted, or to be zealous; the word **πῦρ** (*pur*); is the Greek word for fire; compounded, to enthusiastically, fervently, passionately, vigorously, or zealously rekindle a fire until it burns brightly again; to stir a flame again; to stoke and rekindle the embers of a fire until it is once again burning brightly

4. "spirit" — **πνεῦμα** (*pneuma*): spirit

5. "fear" — **δειλός** (*deilos*): a gripping fear or dread that produces a shrinking back or cowardice; a dread that saps one's ability to look at a problem head-on and causes him to retreat; to be timid or cowardice

6. "power" — **δύναμις** (*dunamis*): power; the idea of explosive, superhuman power that comes with enormous energy and produces phenomenal, extraordinary, and unparalleled results

7. "love" — **ἀγαπη** (*agape*): God's kind of love; high-level love; describes the admiration one had for a person or object; the onlooker was so taken by the object that he couldn't simply look at it, he gazed upon it and became affected by it, even experiencing a loss of words to express the admiration and love for person or object; high-level love; God's kind of love

8. "sound mind" — **σωφρονέω** (*sophroneo*): to be of sound mind; to be reasonable; to be balanced and levelheaded in the way one thinks; to think rationally

9. "but" — **δὲ** (*de*): an exclamatory point

10. "call to remembrance" — **ἀναμιμνήσκω** (*anamimnesko*): a compound that means to repeat, to remember, to remind, to regather, or to recollect memories

11. "former" — **πρότερον** (*proteron*): former; earlier

12. "illuminated" — **φωτίζω** (*photidzo*): to illuminate; the impression of a brilliant flash of light that leaves a permanent and lasting impression

13. "endured" — **ὑπομένω** (*hupomeno*): to stay or abide; to remain in one's spot; to keep a position; to resolve to maintain territory gained; in a military sense, it pictures soldiers ordered to maintain their positions even in the face of opposition; to defiantly stick it out regardless of pressures mounted against it; staying power; hang-in-there power; the attitude that holds out, holds on, outlasts, perseveres, and hangs in there, never giving up, refusing to surrender to obstacles, and turning down every opportunity to quit; pictures one who is under a heavy load but refuses to bend, break, or surrender because he is convinced

that the territory, promise, or principle under assault rightfully belongs to him

14. "great" — **πολλὴν** (*pollen*): great in terms of quantity; many; substantial numbers

15. "fight" — **ἄθλησις** (*athlesis*): an athletic term; denotes a heroic act

16. "afflictions" — **πάθημα** (*pathema*): suffering; a strong emotional struggle; emotional or mental agony

17. "gazingstock" — **θεατρίζω** (*theatridzo*): theater; observe, watch, scrutinize, or bring upon the stage for all to see; pictures spectators in the theater watching a scenario being played before them; on the edge of their seats, spectators wait for the actors to make a mistake or forget a line so they can scorn, ridicule him, and make fun of him; it can be interpreted to bring on to the stage in order to scorn, to scoff at, to shame, sneer at, and to publicly humiliate; spectacle

18. "light" — **ἐλαφρός** (*elaphros*): light; bearable; easily managed

19. "affliction" — **θλῖψις** (*thlipsis*): great pressure; crushing pressure; to suffocate; a horribly tight, life-threatening squeeze; a situation so difficult it causes one to feel stressed, squeezed, pressured, or crushed

20. "moment" — **παραυτίκα** (*parautika*): immediate; for the moment; present; momentary; hence, not long lasting

SYNOPSIS

The emphasis of this lesson:

Pause, turn around, look at your past, and remember how good God has been to you. He carried you through *every* time. Remembering God's goodness will stir your faith so you're ready to conquer the mountain you're facing right now!

The Resurrection of Christ Church in Saint Petersburg, Russia, is also called The Church on Spilled Blood because blood was spilled there in 1881. Czar Alexander II was in his carriage on a road along the canal en route to the Winter Palace when a terrorist threw a bomb under the carriage. It detonated, killed three people, and wounded others — but the Czar (Tsar) himself was basically unharmed.

He emerged from the carriage to see who he could help. When the terrorists saw that he was unharmed, they threw another bomb, which detonated and blew off his legs. He was quickly transported to the Winter Palace, and within several hours he was pronounced dead.

It was a tragedy in the life of Russia. His son, Alexander III, who became the next Czar (Tsar), gave the order for a church to be built on the spot where his father had been mortally wounded: The Resurrection of Christ Church, also called The Church on Spilled Blood. It's known for its marvelous mosaics and for being the site where Alexander II was mortally wounded.

The Power of Remembering God's Goodness to You

Do you ever find your thoughts gravitating toward bad memories? It's easy to remember difficult things that happened to you. But a lot of *good* things have happened in your life! In fact, more *good* things have happened than *bad* things! Human nature tends to remember the bad and forget the good, but you can switch that tendency, and come out on top as a result.

God has been good to you, and *people* have been kind to you and have helped you along in life even when you didn't deserve it. You have been the recipient of *blessing, mercy, favor,* and *kindness.* Be intentional to stop thinking about all the bad things and *remember* all the good things! Psalm 111:4 says, "He hath made his wonderful works to be remembered…." We're not supposed to forget what God has done for us in the past.

"When I call to remembrance the unfeigned faith that is in thee, which dwelt first in thy grandmother Lois, and thy mother Eunice; and I am persuaded that in thee also" (2 Timothy 1:5).

Paul knew, and basically said, "What are you worried about, Timothy? I know your family, and the faith that works in it. God has always been faithful to your family. *Remember,* the same God who was faithful to your grandmother and your mother is faithful to you!"

Timothy was worried about his future. He was facing difficult moments in his life, and he had a spirit of fear. He needed to remember that God had been faithful to him and his family. Paul called to remembrance the "unfeigned faith" that was in Timothy. Rather than look at the word "unfeigned," let's first see what the word "feigned" means. It describes a hypocrite, or someone who is fake — like an actor on a stage who wears a mask. Jesus called the scribes and Pharisee's "hypocrites." So Jesus was saying,

"Your faith is not real, and your prayers are not sincere. You're just performing like actors with masks, playing your part because people are watching."

In essence, Paul said to Timothy, "You *don't* have a hypocritical faith. Your faith is real, and authentic." He was "persuaded," which is the Greek word *peitho*, and means *convinced to the core* or *rock-solid certainty*. Paul was convinced that the same faith that worked in Timothy's grandmother and mother was at work in Timothy, and *everything* was going to turn out all right.

Rekindle The Fire in Your Heart Until It Burns Brightly Again

"Wherefore I put thee in remembrance that thou stir up the gift of God, which is in thee by the putting on of my hands" (2 Timothy 1:6). The Greek text says, "I'm reminding you of these things that *by remembering them* you will stir up the gift of God that is in you." Here we find *the power of memory*. Just like you need a poker to stir the embers to keep a flame burning, memory is like a poker in your hand. When your embers are on a low burn and your fire is about to go out — stir it up again!

In the program Rick shared, "Memory is such a powerful tool in my life. In moments when I feel like I'm on a low burn or I'm facing something that's a little threatening, I put everything on pause, because if you just look at what is in front of you, sometimes it can seem like a mountain that you cannot overcome. But if you'll put it on pause and turn around and look at your past, you will recall that the things you've faced in your past were just as big as what you're facing right now. In fact, they may have been bigger, and God walked you victoriously through every one of them. You survived every one of those attacks; you got through every one of those issues."

"And the same God who walked you through all of those is going to help you overcome the mountain in front of you right now. You just need to stir up your faith by remembering the faithfulness of the Lord."

Timothy's Fire Was on a Low Burn Because He Allowed the Things Around Him To Get to Him

In Second Timothy 1:6, Paul exhorted, "I put thee in remembrance that thou stir up the gift of God, which is in thee…." The words "stir up" is the

Greek word *anadzoopureo*, a compound of *ana*, *zoon*, and *pur*. The word *ana* carries the idea of *repeating an earlier action or doing something again*; the word *zoon* is from a word meaning *to be enthusiastic, to be fervent, to be passionate, to be vigorous, to be wholehearted*, or *to be zealous*; and the word *pur* is the Greek word for *fire*. When you put these words together, they picture *to enthusiastically, fervently, passionately, vigorously, or zealously rekindle a fire until it burns brightly again*. It denotes *to stir a flame again* or *to stoke and rekindle the embers of a fire until it is once again burning brightly*.

Timothy received many negative reports, and they were beginning to dampen his faith. People had walked out on him, and he was concerned about what might happen to him. Paul reminded him that the vibrant faith that lived and took up residency in his grandmother and in his mother lived in him as well.

My friend, a living, vibrant faith dwells in you too! The same God who was faithful to them is faithful to *you* right now. Paul said, "I'm persuaded of it, convinced to the core, rock-solid certain that everything is going to be okay. And I'm reminding you of all this that by you remembering God's faithfulness, you will stir up the gift of God that is in you."

Fear Is a Spirit and Can Cause You To Think Irrationally

"For God hath not given us the spirit of fear; but of power, and of love, and of a sound mind" (2 Timothy 1:7). Again, the word "spirit" is the Greek word *pneuma* and it describes a *spirit* — fear is a spirit. You can feel it when it comes in the room, and you suddenly think irrationally and worry about things that will never happen. It works in your imagination, which can seem so real to you that you lean into fear and panic. The word "fear" is the Greek word *deilos* and depicts *a gripping fear or dread that produces a shrinking back or cowardice*. It's *a dread that saps one's ability to look at a problem head-on and causes him to retreat*. And it also means *timidity* or *cowardice*.

Paul said God has not given you the spirit of fear, but of "...power, love and a sound mind." The word "power" is the Greek word *dunamis*, and carries the idea of *explosive, superhuman power that comes with enormous energy and produces phenomenal, extraordinary, and unparalleled results*. The word "love" is the Greek word *agape* and depicts *God's kind of love*. God has given you a love that overcomes your feelings and your fears.

The Greek word *sophroneo* — translated as "sound mind" — describes *to be of sound mind*; *to be reasonable*; *to be balanced and levelheaded in the way one thinks*; and *to think rationally*. It literally means *a saved brain*. God has given you a mind that is delivered from fear; you have a sound mind that thinks reasonably and not irrationally.

Refuse To Bend, Break, or Surrender — the Promise Under Assault Rightfully *Belongs* to You!

"But call to remembrance the former days, in which, after ye were illuminated, ye endured a great fight of afflictions" (Hebrews 10:32). The writer of Hebrews said you've got to "...call to remembrance...." This means you have to *intentionally* remember the right things.

What are you to remember? "...The former days, in which, after ye were illuminated..." (Hebrews 10:32). The word "illuminated" is the Greek word *photidzo*, and it means *to illuminate*. It pictures *the impression of a brilliant flash of light that leaves a permanent and lasting impression*. Illumination leaves a lasting impression on your life. The writer of Hebrews says, "...after you were illuminated..." after you had this great revelation, you endured a great fight of affliction, which means a fight normally follows illumination. The devil is terrified of people who are illuminated which is why a great fight follows. But the fight will pass! And with the strength of God, you can endure!

The word "endured" is the Greek word *hupomeno*, and it depicts *to stay or abide*; *to remain in one's spot*; *to keep a position*; *to resolve to maintain territory gained*. In a military sense it *pictures soldiers ordered to maintain their positions even in the face of opposition*. It means *to defiantly stick it out regardless of pressures mounted against it*; and pictures *staying power*; and *hang-in-there power*. The word translated "endured" — *hupomeno* — describes *the attitude that holds out, holds on, outlasts, perseveres, and hangs in there, never giving up, refusing to surrender to obstacles, and turning down every opportunity to quit*. It denotes *one who is under a heavy load but refuses to bend, break, or surrender because he is convinced that the territory, promise, or principle under assault rightfully belongs to him*.

You may have to endure a fight, but if you refuse to surrender it *will* pass! And that is why Second Corinthians 4:17 says, "For our light affliction, which is but for a moment...." It's just for a moment. The word "moment" is the Greek word *parautika*, and it describes something that is *immediate*;

for the moment; *present*; *momentary*; and something that is *not long lasting*. When you're facing a challenge that seems like it will never end, realize the Bible says it's *just for a moment, temporary, fleeting*, and *not long lasting*. What is required of you right now is that you endure until it passes.

You Have 'Staying Power'

My friend, it *will* pass! Whatever the mountain is, whatever the issue is that you're facing right now, *you will get through it*! You need staying power until that mountain moves out of the way. And it's important for you to never forget the works of the Lord. "He hath made his wonderful works to be remembered" (Psalm 111:4).

Think about what you've already been through. You survived every single event, and here you are! Based on God's faithfulness to you in the past, you're going to get beyond this situation too! Just remember God's goodness, stir up your faith, and you will overcome the present mountain.

STUDY QUESTIONS

Study to shew thyself approved unto God, a workman that needeth not to be ashamed, rightly dividing the word of truth.
— 2 Timothy 2:15

1. Psalm 111:4 says, "He hath made his wonderful works to be remembered: the Lord is gracious and full of compassion." As we learned in this lesson, we are *to call to remembrance* (remember and think about) His wonderful works and stir up the gift of God that is in us. Where are some examples of *recalling His mighty works* in the Bible? (*See* Deuteronomy 3:24; Psalm 145:4-13; and Psalm 78:4-7.)

2. "...They forgot His works, and the wonders that He had shown them" (Psalm 78:11 *ESV*). Continue reading Psalm 78:12-21, and 42 and think about all that God did, yet what was Israel's response? We must never forget the goodness of the Lord and all He has done for us. As our faith is strengthened by remembering His goodness, how can we pass the glorious testimonies of His mighty works on to future generations? (*Consider* Psalm 71:17 and 18 *ESV*.)

PRACTICAL APPLICATION

**But be ye doers of the word, and not hearers only,
deceiving your own selves.**
—James 1:22

1. Second Timothy 1:6 exhorts, "Wherefore I put thee in remembrance that thou stir up the gift of God, which is in thee by the putting on of my hands." The Greek text says, "I'm reminding you of these things that by remembering them you will stir up the gift of God that is in you." It is amazing that memories of His faithfulness can literally rekindle the fire in your heart! Take time right now to recall at least 10 things He brought you through victoriously in the past. Now thank Him in advance for bringing you through your present situation victoriously too!

2. You will outlast and overcome whatever you're facing today! Spend some additional time thinking about the significance of the word "endure" which means to:

- Stay or abide; to remain in one's spot; to keep a position.

- Resolve to maintain territory gained. In a military sense, it pictures soldiers ordered to maintain their positions even in the face of opposition.

- To defiantly stick it out regardless of pressures mounted against it.

- Staying power; hang-in-there power.

- The attitude that holds out, holds on, outlasts, perseveres, and hangs in there, never giving up, refusing to surrender to obstacles, and turning down every opportunity to quit.

- One who is under a heavy load but refuses to bend, break, or surrender because he is convinced that the territory, promise, or principle under assault rightfully belongs to him.

TOPIC

Never Forget God's Promises

SCRIPTURES

1. **Psalm 77:11** — I will remember the works of the Lord: surely I will remember thy wonders of old.

2. **Psalm 143:5** — I remember the days of old; I meditate on all thy works; I muse on the work of thy hands.

3. **2 Timothy 1:5** — When I call to remembrance the unfeigned faith that is in thee, which dwelt first in thy grandmother Lois, and thy mother Eunice; and I am persuaded that in thee also.

4. **2 Timothy 1:6** — Wherefore I put thee in remembrance that thou stir up the gift of God, which is in thee by the putting on of my hands.

5. **2 Timothy 1:7** — For God hath not given us the spirit of fear; but of power, and of love, and of a sound mind.

6. **1 Timothy 1:18** — This charge I commit unto thee, son Timothy, according to the prophecies which went before on thee, that thou by them mightest war a good warfare.

7. **1 Timothy 4:14** — Neglect not the gift that is in thee, which was given thee by prophecy, with the laying on of the hands of the presbytery.

8. GREEK WORDS

9. "unfeigned" — ἀνυπόκριτος (*anupokritos*): authentic; genuine compared to what is pretended, simulated, faked, feigned, or phony; one who is authentic, sincere, or trustworthy; not hypocritical

10. "dwelt" — ἐνοικέω (*enoikeo*): to dwell in a house; to take up residency; to settle into a home; to be at home; to be a permanent indweller

11. "I put thee in remembrance" — ἀναμιμνήσκω (*anamimnesko*): a compound that means to repeat, to remember, to remind, to regather, or to recollect memories

12. "stir up" — ἀναζωπυρέω (*anadzoopureo*): compound of ἀνά (*ana*), ζῷον (*zoon*), and πῦρ (*pur*); the word ἀνά (*ana*) carries the idea of repeating an earlier action or doing something again; the word ζῷον

(*zoon*) is from a word meaning to be enthusiastic, to be fervent, to be passionate, to be vigorous, to be wholehearted, or to be zealous; and the word **πῦρ** (*pur*) is the Greek word for fire; compounded, to enthusiastically, fervently, passionately, vigorously, or zealously rekindle a fire until it burns brightly again; to stir a flame again; to stoke and rekindle the embers of a fire until it is once again burning brightly

13. "spirit" — **πνεῦμα** (*pneuma*): spirit

14. "fear" — **δειλός** (*deilos*): a gripping fear or dread that produces a shrinking back or cowardice; a dread that saps one's ability to look at a problem head-on and causes him to retreat; to be timid or cowardice

15. "power" — **δύναμις** (*dunamis*): power; the idea of explosive, superhuman power that comes with enormous energy and produces phenomenal, extraordinary, and unparalleled results

16. "love" — **ἀγαπη** (*agape*): God's kind of love; high-level love

17. "sound mind" — **σωφρονέω** (*sophroneo*): to be of sound mind; to be reasonable; to be balanced and levelheaded in the way one thinks; to think rationally

18. "prophecies" — **προφητεία** (*propheteia*): from **πρό** (*pro*) and **φημί** (*phemi*); the word **πρό** (*pro*) means before and **φημί** (*phemi*) means to speak; to speak in advance of; to foretell; to reveal the mind of God to a person or congregation

19. "went before" — **προάγω** (*proago*): precede; to lead in front of; to lead forward; points toward a leading into the future

20. "on" — **ἐπί** (*epi*): upon

21. "that" — **ἵνα** (*hina*): in order that; pointing to a purpose

22. "by them" — **ἐν αὐταῖς** (*en autais*): literally, in them

23. "mightiest war" — **στρατεύομαι** (*strateuomai*): a strategic act of warfare; deciding a line of attack, what methods to use, including the approach that one charts in advance to conduct a well-thought-out assault

24. "good" — **καλός** (*kalos*): good or useful; refers to what is noble; frequently used to denote good, noble actions, or superior behavior; exceptional, of the highest quality, outstanding, suitable, or superb

25. "warfare" — **στρατεία** (*strateia*): a campaign; military expedition; warfare strategically carried out; where we get the word strategy

26. "neglect not" — **ἀμελέω** (*ameleo*): from **μέλει** (*melei*) with an *a* attached to the front of it;

27. μέλει (*melei*), to be concerned, thoughtful, interested, aware, noticing, and it can depict meticulous attention; when an *a* is attached to the front, it becomes ἀμελέω (*ameleo*), unconcerned, unthoughtful, disinterested, unaware; lacking attention, or neglectful

28. "gift" — χάρισμα (*charisma*): a grace-given gift; derived from χάρις (*charis*), grace; when it becomes χάρισμα (*charisma*): something that is given or imparted by grace; this word was used to describe a moment when the gods graced or donated supernatural ability, favor, or power to an individual; thus, this word meant a gracious gift; a person who has received a charisma has received a donation or an enablement from God that equips him in some supernatural manner

29. "by prophecy" — διὰ προφητείας (*dia propheteias*): literally, through prophecy; with the accompaniment of prophecy

SYNOPSIS

The emphasis of this lesson:

Never forget the wonderful things God *did* for you, *said* to you, and *promised* you personally. If you will grab hold of the promises and the prophecies He has spoken on your life, by them you can wage a good warfare and fulfill His glorious plan for you!

The foundation for the Peter and Paul Cathedral in Saint Petersburg, Russia, was first laid in 1712. It was designed to be the burial place for members of the Romanov dynasty — the former Russian Royal Family — beginning from the time of Peter the Great. The amazing graves of Peter the Great and his wife, Peter III and his wife (who became the legendary Catherine the Great), and many others are in this remarkable cathedral.

In 1992, this was a dark, dreary, and abandoned cathedral because the Soviet regime did not celebrate their imperial history. But today it is very celebrated, and people visit the cathedral because it is filled with history that we should *never forget*.

There are many scriptures that tell us to *call to remembrance* the things God has done for us. Perhaps God did some notable things in *your* life that you have forgotten. You didn't mean to forget, it's just that time passed, other things happened, and you forgot. We are commanded in the Word to *never forget* the works of the Lord. When you *remember* all the mighty things God did for you, it gives you a platform to believe He will be faithful to you again in your future.

The Power of Intentionally *Remembering* the Works of the Lord

Psalm 77:11 says, "I will remember the works of the Lord: surely I will remember thy wonders of old." The phrase "I will" means *you need to be deliberate — I will intentionally remember* the works of the Lord; *I will intentionally choose to remember.* Similarly, Psalm 143:5 says, "I remember the days of old; I meditate on all thy works; I muse on the work of thy hands." When you remember what God has done for you in the past, it bolsters your faith to overcome what you're facing right now.

Paul wrote to Timothy, "When I call to remembrance the unfeigned faith that is in thee, which dwelt first in thy grandmother Lois, and thy mother Eunice; and I am persuaded that in thee also. Wherefore I put thee in remembrance that thou stir up the gift of God, which is in thee by the putting on of my hands. For God hath not given us the spirit of fear; but of power, and of love, and of a sound mind" (2 Timothy 1:5-7). When Paul wrote these verses, Timothy was in a bad place and feared for his future. So Paul reminded him of a few things.

The Greek word *anupokritos* — translated "unfeigned" — describes something *authentic or genuine* compared to what is simulated, fake, feigned, or phony. It depicts one who is *authentic, sincere, or trustworthy; not hypocritical.* In contrast, the word "feigned" describes *hypocrites,* and the word "hypocrite" describes *actors on the stage in the ancient world who wore masks.* They "feigned" a mask and pretended to be what they were not. They were just actors on the stage playing a part for others to see. They were not authentic; they were phony.

A Real Living Faith Is at Work in You!

Paul used the word "unfeigned" to say, "Timothy, your faith is *not* fake. You're *not* a pretender; you're *the real deal;* you have an unfeigned faith in you which dwelt first in your grandmother Lois and your mother Eunice…." The word "dwelt," translated from the Greek word *enoikeo,* means *to dwell in a house; to take up residency; to settle into a home; to be at home;* or *to be a permanent indweller.* It was the equivalent of saying, "Faith was real in your grandmother, and it was real in your mother. Faith *lived* in them, and it took up *residency* in them. And I'm persuaded this same faith is at work in *you* as well!"

Paul continued in his letter to Timothy, "Wherefore I put thee in remembrance that thou stir up the gift of God, which is in thee by the putting on of my hands" (2 Timothy 1:6). When you read this in the Greek text it says it differently — in an important way. The Greek literally says, "I'm reminding you of all these things that *by remembering them* thou might stir up the gift of God that is in thee by the putting on of my hands."

The Greek word *anadzoopureo* — translated as "stir up" — is a compound of *ana, zoon,* and *pur.* The word *ana* carries the idea of *repeating an earlier action or doing something again*; the word *zoon* is from a word meaning *to be enthusiastic, to be fervent, to be passionate, to be vigorous, to be wholehearted, or to be zealous*; and the word *pur* is the Greek word for fire. Compounded, the word *anadzoopureo,* translated as "stir up" means *to enthusiastically, fervently, passionately, vigorously, or zealously rekindle a fire until it burns brightly again.* It pictures *to stir a flame again; to stoke and rekindle the embers of a fire until it is once again burning brightly.*

The very fact that Paul used this word meant Timothy's fire was on a low burn, and the embers were about to go out. In essence, Paul said, "Timothy, I'm going to tell you how to stoke the coals in your own heart. You need to *remember*." This is the "stoker" that God has put in every person's hand: Put everything on pause and intentionally remember a few things.

Paul said, "I'm reminding you of all these things that by *your remembering* you will stir up again the gift of God that is in you." And in that same way, *you* can stir the embers of your heart and get the fire burning again. Stop, look at your past, and remember all the impossible things you have faced: Sickness, financial problems, and attacks of the enemy. God walked you through every one of them! In the past, perhaps you didn't think you'd get through those things — but you did! And here you are!

Remember all the moments God miraculously moved in your life and replay them in your mind over and over. By the time you recall all those things you walked through and thanked God for His faithfulness, what you're facing right now won't look so big after all!

The Spirit of Fear Must Be Resisted

Second Timothy 1:7 says, "For God hath not given us the spirit of fear; but of power, and of love, and of a sound mind." The Greek word *pneuma* — translated as "spirit" describes a *spirit*. Fear is a *spiritual* force. You can feel it when it comes in the room; it may cause worry or even panic. Fear is a *spirit*, and it must be resisted.

The Greek word *deilos* — translated as "fear" — describes *a gripping fear or dread that produces a shrinking back or cowardice*. It denotes *a dread that saps one's ability to look at a problem head on and causes him to retreat, to be timid, or cowardice*. In essence Paul said, "God did not give you something that would produce dread in you. Instead, He has given you *power, love, and a sound mind*."

The word "power" is the Greek word *dunamis,* and pictures *power*. It carries the idea of *explosive, superhuman power that comes with enormous energy and produces phenomenal, extraordinary, and unparalleled results*. It depicts *a force of nature,* like an earthquake or tsunami. It was the word used by the Roman army to describe *the full might of an advancing army*. Paul said, "God has given you the Holy Ghost, and He will turn you into a supernatural force of nature. You'll shake things up, and the power in you will drive back the spirit of fear."

Paul goes on to say, "…and of love, and of a sound mind." The Greek word *sophroneo* — translated as "sound mind" — is a compound of two words: The first word means to be *saved, healed,* or *delivered*. And the second is the word for *your brain* or *intelligence*. When these two words are compounded, it forms the word *sophroneo* and means *to be of sound mind*; *to be reasonable*; *to be balanced and levelheaded in the way one thinks*; and *to think rationally*. It pictures *a delivered head* or *saved brains*. God has given you *saved brains*! He delivered your head, so there is no need to dread the present or the future. God wants you to think rationally. When you're irrational, a spirit of fear is at work.

Remember the Words God Has Spoken to You

"This charge I commit unto thee, son Timothy, according to the prophecies which went before on thee, that thou by them mightest war a good warfare" (1 Timothy 1:18). We need to remember the words God has spoken to us. Paul said, I give you this charge "…according to the prophecies...." The word "prophecy" — the Greek word *propheteia* — is from the word *pro* and the word *phemi*. The word *pro* means *before* and *phemi* means *to speak*. When combined, they form *propheteia*, meaning *to speak in advance of*, *to foretell*; and *to reveal the mind of God to a person or congregation*.

Paul, in essence said, "Timothy, God has spoken to you about your future. He's told you how He's going to use you. Remember the prophecies that have been spoken to you. God foretold what He wants to do with your life." The Greek word *proago* — translated as "went before" — means *to precede*; *to lead in front of*, *to lead forward*; and it points toward *a leading into the future*. The word *on* is a translation of the Greek word *epi*, which means *upon*. It conveys a word from God that fell *on* you.

The word "that" in Greek is the word *hina*, and it *points to a purpose*. Paul said, "Here's the purpose of the prophecies: If you grab hold of them, by them (the Greek actually says *in them*) you will war a good warfare." When God speaks a word to you, begin to soak it up and become saturated in it. Paul admonished Timothy, "Don't forget what God said to you and promised you. You need to be *in* those words, *surrounded* by those words, and *soaking up* those words until they are *in* you." Why? That by them thou "...mightest war a good warfare."

Prophecies That Go Before You Give You Direction To Chart Your Future By

The Greek word *strateuomai* — translated as "mightiest war" — depicts *a strategic act of warfare*. It pictures *deciding a line of attack*, and *what methods to use, including the approach that one charts in advance to conduct a well-thought-out assault*. When God gives you direction through a promise or a prophecy, it gives you the ability to chart out your future. That's *why* God speaks to you in advance. Prophecies that go before you give you direction; they tell you what God wants to do in your life.

If you can fight a *good* warfare, that means it's also possible to fight a *bad* warfare. If you forget what God said to you, your warfare will lack substance. But if you *remember* and fight according to what *God said* to you, you can wage a good warfare.

The word "good" is the Greek word *kalos*, which describes something that is *good or useful*. It is frequently used to denote *good, noble actions*, or *superior behavior, exceptional, of the highest quality, outstanding, suitable, or superb.* When you have a word from God, it puts you in a superior position. In fact, it enables you to fight a good "warfare" — the Greek word *strateia* — which describes *a campaign, a military expedition, a warfare strategically carried out.* It's where we get the word "strategy."

In the program, Rick shared, "In my own life God has spoken to me and has told me very important things. Those words have given me direction and helped me to form a strategy for what actions I'm to take, what I'm supposed to do, and sometimes what I'm *not* supposed to do. When God speaks to you it gives you direction for your life and enables you to chart your future."

When prophecies go before you — foretelling what God wants to do through you — they give you direction for your life. Timothy was in a bad situation, and he was looking at all the terrible events happening to him because of the persecution raging all around him. He was tempted to think his future was going to be aborted.

In essence Paul said, "Timothy, your mother and your grandmother had a real living faith, and that same authentic faith is in you! God did not give you the spirit of fear that's causing you to dread the future. God gave you power, love, and a sound mind. He gave you a promise, and He gave you prophecies which you need to hold onto and fight according to. If you'll hold onto them, and chart your life by them, you'll be able to wage a good warfare."

And so will *you*, my friend!

STUDY QUESTIONS

Study to shew thyself approved unto God, a workman that needeth not to be ashamed, rightly dividing the word of truth.
— 2 Timothy 2:15

1. According to Second Timothy 1:7, a spirit of fear doesn't come from God, so where does it come from? Rather than passively suffering under the spirit of fear's influence, we are to *resist* it. What does First Peter 5:8-9 and James 4:7 teach us to do regarding the devil?

2. When the Holy Spirit within you bears witness regarding a prophecy and it lines up with the Word of God, embrace it wholeheartedly, and

as we learned in this lesson, wage a strategic warfare with it! What does First Thessalonians 5:21 instruct you to do?

3. According to First Corinthians 14:3, what are three elements that are present when a prophecy comes forth by the Holy Spirit?

PRACTICAL APPLICATION

> But be ye doers of the word, and not hearers only,
> deceiving your own selves.
> — James 1:22

1. **Prophecy**

   Take a moment to read First Corinthians 14:29-33,40 and notice the instruction the Holy Spirit gives us about prophecy. Are there prophecies you received in the past that you need to pull out and read again? Realize they are strategic in the plan of God for your life and are to be honored. Lift them to the Lord as you pray today, and by faith *lay hold* of them!

2. **Promises**

   Just like your body needs three good meals a day to function at its best, your spirit needs to be fed well every day. Physically, you can't survive on one small meal a week, and spiritually you can't thrive reading God's Word once a week. Hunger after Him and feed your spirit daily by reading His Word! As you do, specific verses will stand out to you and become illuminated in your spirit. When that happens, write them down, memorize them, and meditate on them. Realize that God is speaking to you and promising you something very specific. And that, my friend, is glorious! (Consider Second Timothy 3:16; and the following verses in Psalm 119 — 9, 11, 16, 25, 28, 41-43, 49, 50, 74, 89, 101, 103, 105, 107, 114, 116, 130, 140, 148, 154, 162, 170, and 172.)

TOPIC

Never Forget To Build Markers To Recall What God Has Done

SCRIPTURES

1. **Deuteronomy 6:12** — Then beware lest thou forget the Lord, which brought thee forth out of the land of Egypt, from the house of bondage.

2. **Deuteronomy 8:11-17** — Beware that thou forget not the Lord thy God, in not keeping his commandments, and his judgments, and his statutes, which I command thee this day: Lest when thou hast eaten and art full, and hast built goodly houses, and dwelt therein; And when thy herds and thy flocks multiply, and thy silver and thy gold is multiplied, and all that thou hast is multiplied; Then thine heart be lifted up, and thou forget the Lord thy God, which brought thee forth out of the land of Egypt, from the house of bondage; Who led thee through that great and terrible wilderness, wherein were fiery serpents, and scorpions, and drought, where there was no water; who brought thee forth water out of the rock of flint; Who fed thee in the wilderness with manna, which thy fathers knew not, that he might humble thee, and that he might prove thee, to do thee good at thy latter end; And thou say in thine heart, My power and the might of mine hand hath gotten me this wealth.

3. **Deuteronomy 8:18** — But thou shalt remember the Lord thy God: for it is he that giveth thee power to get wealth, that he may establish his covenant which he sware unto thy fathers, as it is this day.

4. **Deuteronomy 8:19** — And it shall be, if thou do at all forget the Lord thy God, and walk after other gods, and serve them, and worship them, I testify against you this day that ye shall surely perish.

5. **Deuteronomy 32:7** — Remember the days of old, consider the years of many generations: ask thy father, and he will shew thee; thy elders, and they will tell thee.

6. **Genesis 28:10-16** — And Jacob went out from Beersheba, and went toward Haran. And he lighted upon a certain place, and tarried there all night, because the sun was set; and he took of the stones of that

place, and put them for his pillows, and lay down in that place to sleep. And he dreamed, and behold a ladder set up on the earth, and the top of it reached to heaven: and behold the angels of God ascending and descending on it. And, behold, the Lord stood above it, and said, I am the Lord God of Abraham thy father, and the God of Isaac: the land whereon thou liest, to thee will I give it, and to thy seed; And thy seed shall be as the dust of the earth, and thou shalt spread abroad to the west, and to the east, and to the north, and to the south: and in thee and in thy seed shall all the families of the earth be blessed. And, behold, I am with thee, and will keep thee in all places whither thou goest, and will bring thee again into this land; for I will not leave thee, until I have done that which I have spoken to thee of. And Jacob awaked out of his sleep, and he said, Surely the Lord is in this place; and I knew it not.

7. **Genesis 28:18,19** — And Jacob rose up early in the morning, and took the stone that he had put for his pillows, and set it up for a pillar, and poured oil upon the top of it. And he called the name of that place Bethel….

8. **Joshua 4:1-9** — And it came to pass, when all the people were clean passed over Jordan, that the Lord spake unto Joshua, saying, Take you twelve men out of the people, out of every tribe a man, and command ye them, saying, Take you hence out of the midst of Jordan, out of the place where the priests' feet stood firm, twelve stones, and ye shall carry them over with you, and leave them in the lodging place, where ye shall lodge this night. Then Joshua called the twelve men, whom he had prepared of the children of Israel, out of every tribe a man: And Joshua said unto them, Pass over before the ark of the Lord your God into the midst of Jordan, and take you up every man of you a stone upon his shoulder, according unto the number of the tribes of the children of Israel: That this may be a sign among you, that when your children ask their fathers in time to come, saying, What mean ye by these stones? Then ye shall answer them, That the waters of Jordan were cut off before the ark of the covenant of the Lord; when it passed over Jordan, the waters of Jordan were cut off: and these stones shall be for a memorial unto the children of Israel forever. And the children of Israel did so as Joshua commanded, and took up twelve stones out of the midst of Jordan, as the Lord spake unto Joshua, according to the number of the tribes of the children of Israel, and carried them over with them unto the place where they lodged, and

laid them down there. And Joshua set up twelve stones in the midst of Jordan, in the place where the feet of the priests which bare the ark of the covenant stood: and they are there unto this day.

9. **1 Samuel 7:7-12** — And when the Philistines heard that the children of Israel were gathered together to Mizpeh, the lords of the Philistines went up against Israel. And when the children of Israel heard it, they were afraid of the Philistines. And the children of Israel said to Samuel, Cease not to cry unto the Lord our God for us, that he will save us out of the hand of the Philistines. And Samuel took a sucking lamb, and offered it for a burnt offering wholly unto the Lord: and Samuel cried unto the Lord for Israel; and the Lord heard him. And as Samuel was offering up the burnt offering, the Philistines drew near to battle against Israel: but the Lord thundered with a great thunder on that day upon the Philistines, and discomfited them; and they were smitten before Israel. And the men of Israel went out of Mizpeh, and pursued the Philistines, and smote them, until they came under Bethcar. Then Samuel took a stone, and set it between Mizpeh and Shen, and called the name of it Ebenezer, saying, Hitherto hath the Lord helped us.

10. **Psalm 77:11** — I will remember the works of the Lord: surely I will remember thy wonders of old.

GREEK WORDS

There are no Greek words for this lesson.

SYNOPSIS

The emphasis of this lesson:

God has done so many wondrous works in your life! Discover the power of remembering the marvelous works of God by building markers and memorials so you will *never forget* what He has done for you.

The Cathedral of Peter and Paul in Saint Petersburg, Russia, is where all the members of the Romanov dynasty are buried with the exception of two. In one of the cathedral's rooms, the last ruling Romanov family is buried. They were shot in the basement of the Ipatiev House in Yekaterinburg on July 17, 1918. That night they were told to get up and get dressed because they were going to be taken to the basement where a family photo would be taken. They were expecting photographers, but instead, soldiers came in with guns, shot them, and discarded their bodies in a local forest.

Decades later, their bodies were found, and on July 17, 1998, 80 years after their execution, they were officially buried in the Cathedral of Peter and Paul. The whole family was buried with the exception of Maria and Alexi, whose bodies were found later. Today, the bodies are in Moscow in a laboratory waiting to finally be buried.

This was a remarkable family, and they were killed horribly in Yekaterinburg in 1918. Today, the Cathedral of Peter and Paul is very special to the Russian people because they want to *never forget* this precious family and what happened to them. Likewise, it's important for you to build markers in your life commemorating key moments and events *you* should *never forget*.

If God Did It Before, He'll Do It Again

If you're fearful about your future, perhaps you've forgotten the wondrous works the Lord did for you in the past. Think about all the challenging things you've already faced in life. You walked through every one of those events because God was *with* you.

Put everything on pause, turn around and look at your past, and you will see how God walked with you through every single challenge! Jesus was faithful to you in the past, and He never changes! Hebrews 13:8 says, "Jesus Christ the same yesterday, and today, and forever." If He did it before, He'll do it again in your life!

According to Second Timothy 1:6, as you remember God's faithfulness you stir up the gift of God that is in you. Paul said, "I'm reminding you of all these things that by remembering them you might stir up the gift of God that is in you." Remembering helps you stir the embers in your heart so the fire inside you will burn brightly again, and you'll be ready to face today's challenges.

Psalm 77:11 declares, "I will remember the works of the Lord: surely I will remember thy wonders of old." Notice it says, "I will" twice. You have to intentionally *choose* to remember. If you don't choose to remember, life gets busy, and you may forget the wonderful things God did for you.

In the program, Rick shared, "There are events in my life that are so profound that I've built markers on the calendar — like monuments to me — so I always remember what happened on that day. When I come to those dates I stop, I pause, and I reflect on what happened. Every time we begin a new building project, or God asks us to do something by faith, before I launch out into new territory, I stop to remember how God enabled us to take past territory. When we faced giants, and giant after giant fell, and God enabled us to take that territory, it's like a monument or a marker in my mind that I want to never forget."

'Beware, Lest Thou Forget'

Deuteronomy 6:12 says, "Then beware lest thou forget the Lord, which brought thee forth out of the land of Egypt, from the house of bondage." How could you ever forget all that God has done for you?

"Beware that thou forget not the Lord thy God, in not keeping his commandments, and his judgments, and his statutes, which I command thee this day: Lest when thou hast eaten and art full, and hast built goodly houses, and dwelt therein; And when thy herds and thy flocks multiply, and thy silver and thy gold is multiplied, and all that thou hast is multiplied; Then thine heart be lifted up, and thou forget the Lord thy God, which brought thee forth out of the land of Egypt, from the house of bondage; Who led thee through that great and terrible wilderness, wherein were fiery serpents, and scorpions, and drought, where there was no water; who brought thee forth water out of the rock of flint; Who fed thee in the wilderness with manna, which thy fathers knew not, that he might humble thee, and that he might prove thee, to do thee good at thy latter end; And thou say in thine heart, My power and the might of mine hand hath gotten me this wealth" (Deuteronomy 8:11-17).

Never forget what God has done for you! You did not do this by yourself — the hand of God went to work on your behalf. He brought you forth, delivered you, gave you a good beginning, and has a glorious future for you.

In Deuteronomy 8:18,19 we're told, "But thou shalt remember the Lord thy God: for it is he that giveth thee power to get wealth, that he may establish his covenant which he sware unto thy fathers, as it is this day. And it shall be, if thou do at all forget the Lord thy God, and walk after other gods, and serve them, and worship them, I testify against you this day that ye shall surely perish." If we forget we are recipients of the mercy of God, it opens the door for bad things to happen.

Tell your children and your grandchildren about the wonderful things God has done in your life! Deuteronomy 32:7 declares, "Remember the days of old, consider the years of many generations: ask thy father, and he will shew thee; thy elders, and they will tell thee."

Build Monuments or Markers To *Remember*

Example One:
Bethel — The House of God

Our first example of a child of God building a monument to mark and remember God's faithfulness is found in Genesis 28:10-15 which says, "And Jacob went out from Beersheba, and went toward Haran. And he lighted upon a certain place, and tarried there all night, because the sun was set; and he took of the stones of that place, and put them for his pillows, and lay down in that place to sleep."

"And he dreamed, and behold a ladder set up on the earth, and the top of it reached to heaven: and behold the angels of God ascending and descending on it. And, behold, the Lord stood above it, and said, I am the Lord God of Abraham thy father, and the God of Isaac: the land whereon thou liest, to thee will I give it, and to thy seed; And thy seed shall be as the dust of the earth, and thou shalt spread abroad to the west, and to the east, and to the north, and to the south: and in thee and in thy seed shall all the families of the earth be blessed. And, behold, I am with thee, and will keep thee in all places whither thou goest, and will bring thee again into this land; for I will not leave thee, until I have done that which I have spoken to thee of."

Genesis 28:16-19 continues, "And Jacob awaked out of his sleep, and he said, Surely the Lord is in this place; and I knew it not. And he was afraid, and said, How dreadful is this place! This is none other but the house of God, and this is the gate of heaven. And Jacob rose up early in the morning, and took the stone that he had put for his pillows, and set it up for a pillar, and poured oil upon the top of it. And he called the name of that place Bethel...."

"Bethel" means *God is in this place*, or *this is the house of God.* Jacob set up a marker — a memorial — to commemorate what God did in that place. He wanted to *never forget* his experience with the power and the glory of God that happened there, so he did something to *commemorate* it.

Example Two:
Gilgal — Where the Waters of Jordan Were Cut Off

Our second example of building monuments or markers to remember what God has done took place when Joshua led the people of Israel across the Jordan River. Joshua 4:1-3 recounts, "And it came to pass, when all the people were clean passed over Jordan, that the Lord spake unto Joshua, saying, Take you twelve men out of the people, out of every tribe a man, And command ye them, saying, Take you hence out of the midst of Jordan, out of the place where the priests' feet stood firm, twelve stones, and ye shall carry them over with you, and leave them in the lodging place, where ye shall lodge this night."

Joshua 4:4-7 continues, "Then Joshua called the twelve men, whom he had prepared of the children of Israel, out of every tribe a man: And Joshua said unto them, Pass over before the ark of the Lord your God into the midst of Jordan, and take you up every man of you a stone upon his shoulder, according unto the number of the tribes of the children of Israel: That this may be a sign among you, that when your children ask their fathers in time to come, saying, What mean ye by these stones? Then ye shall answer them, That the waters of Jordan were cut off before the ark of the covenant of the Lord; when it passed over Jordan, the waters of Jordan were cut off: and these stones shall be for a memorial unto the children of Israel forever."

"And the children of Israel did so as Joshua commanded, and took up twelve stones out of the midst of Jordan, as the Lord spake unto Joshua, according to the number of the tribes of the children of Israel, and carried them over with them unto the place where they lodged, and laid them down there. And Joshua set up twelve stones in the midst of Jordan, in the place where the feet of the priests which bare the ark of the covenant stood: and they are there unto this day" (Joshua 4:8,9).

The Bible tells us the purpose of the stones: They were to be testaments of what God did in that place. Joshua basically said, "In the future, when your children ask what these stones are, you are to remind them that this is where we supernaturally crossed the Jordan because God mightily moved in our midst." They created a memorial — a marker — to commemorate what God had done in their lives.

Example Three:
Ebenezer — The Stone of Help

Our third example of memorials established to help people remember what God did is found in First Samuel 7:7 and 8, which says, "And when the Philistines heard that the children of Israel were gathered together to Mizpeh, the lords of the Philistines went up against Israel. And when the children of Israel heard it, they were afraid of the Philistines. And the children of Israel said to Samuel, Cease not to cry unto the Lord our God for us, that he will save us out of the hand of the Philistines."

"And Samuel took a sucking lamb, and offered it for a burnt offering wholly unto the Lord: and Samuel cried unto the Lord for Israel; and the Lord heard him. And as Samuel was offering up the burnt offering, the Philistines drew near to battle against Israel: but the Lord thundered with a great thunder on that day upon the Philistines, and discomfited them; and they were smitten before Israel. And the men of Israel went out of Mizpeh, and pursued the Philistines, and smote them, until they came under Beth-car. Then Samuel took a stone, and set it between Mizpeh and Shen, and called the name of it Ebenezer, saying, Hitherto hath the Lord helped us" (1 Samuel 7:9-12).

Ebenezer means *the stone of help,* and it was set up by Samuel to mark and remember where God helped Israel to defeat the Philistines. It proclaimed, "…hitherto hath the Lord helped us."

What Have You Done To Commemorate and Remember Key Things God Has Done in *Your* Life?

In all three examples, people wanted to *never forget* — so they did something to help them remember what God did at key moments in their lives. What about you? What are you doing to remember key moments in which God has done something significant in your life?

What has God done for you? Have you forgotten, or have you done something to permanently memorialize and commemorate it? There are many ways to build markers and memorials. For example, you can celebrate the anniversary of the date you were saved. Put it on the calendar and say, "This is the day God saved me!" Tell your children and your grandchildren about the marvelous works of the Lord in your life. Intentionally do something special on that date annually to remember the works of the Lord.

Again, Psalm 77:11 says, "I will remember the works of the Lord: surely I will remember thy wonders of old." As you remember, you stir up the gift of God on the inside of you, and your faith burns brightly. Rest assured, God performed wonderful works in your life in the past, and He will do it again both now and in the future because Jesus Christ is the same yesterday, today, and forever!

STUDY QUESTIONS

> Study to shew thyself approved unto God, a workman that needeth
> not to be ashamed, rightly dividing the word of truth.
> — 2 Timothy 2:15

1. "And he took bread, and gave thanks, and brake it, and gave unto them, saying, This is my body which is given for you: this do in remembrance of me" (Luke 22:19). What does communion help us remember? (*Consider* First Corinthians 11:24-26.)

2. How many times does Peter refer to *remembering* in Second Peter 1:12-15? Why did he emphasize remembering? Peter took the opportunity to "…stir you up by putting you into remembrance…." According to Second Peter 1:12, what is it that remembering establishes us in?

3. Who is it that brings all things to our remembrance? (*See* John 14:26.)

PRACTICAL APPLICATION

> But be ye doers of the word, and not hearers only,
> deceiving your own selves.
> — James 1:22

1. To apply the truths in this lesson, set up some markers and memorials so you never forget the many wonders the Lord has already done in your life. Here are some creative ways to *remember* God's goodness.

   • Take time to add memorable dates like your salvation, restoration, or healing to your calendar and celebrate them with your family each year.

- People make "vision boards" about their dreams for the future. Why not make a "Look What the Lord Has Done" bulletin board and put pictures with descriptive words to commemorate God's works in your life! Every time you see it, thank God for His goodness toward you, and allow your faith to soar regarding the things you are facing now.

- Create a "Victory Wall" in your home where you can frame individual pictures of marked moments that display God's goodness in the history of your family. These are tangible reminders of the goodness of God in your life!

2. What are you facing in your life right now? Take a moment to recall your past circumstances and intentionally remember how God brought you through to the place of victory in similar situations. Now take time to praise Him by faith that you'll come out of this present circumstance victoriously too! (*Consider* Psalm 100:4 and Psalm 145:4 and 5.)

LESSON 5

TOPIC

Never Forget People God Has Used To Be a Blessing to You

SCRIPTURES

1. **2 Timothy 1:15** — This thou knowest, that all they which are in Asia be turned away from me; of whom are Phygellus and Hermogenes.

2. **2 Timothy 1:16** — The Lord give mercy unto the house of Onesiphorus; for he oft refreshed me, and was not ashamed of my chain.

3. **2 Timothy 1:17** — But, when he was in Rome, he sought me out very diligently, and found me.

4. **2 Timothy 1:18** — The Lord grant unto him that he may find mercy of the Lord in that day: and in how many things he ministered unto me at Ephesus, thou knowest very well.

5. **2 Timothy 4:9** — Do thy diligence to come shortly unto me.

6. **2 Timothy 4:10** — For Demas hath forsaken me, having loved this present world, and is departed unto Thessalonica; Crescens to Galatia, Titus unto Dalmatia.
7. **Colossians 4:14** — Luke, the beloved physician, and Demas, greet you.
8. **2 Timothy 4:11** — Only Luke is with me. Take Mark, and bring him with thee: for he is profitable to me for the ministry.
9. **2 Timothy 4:12** — And Tychicus have I sent to Ephesus.
10. **2 Timothy 4:13** — The cloak that I left at Troas with Carpus, when thou comest, bring with thee, and the books, but especially the parchments.
11. **2 Timothy 4:16** — At my first answer no man stood with me, but all men forsook me: I pray God that it may not be laid to their charge.
12. **2 Timothy 4:17** — Notwithstanding the Lord stood with me, and strengthened me; that by me the preaching might be fully known, and that all the Gentiles might hear: and I was delivered out of the mouth of the lion.
13. **Psalm 103:2** — Bless the Lord, O my soul, and forget not all his benefits.

GREEK WORDS

1. "all" — πάντες (*pantes*): all, leaving no one out; all-inclusive
2. "be turned away" — ἀποστρέφω (*apostrepho*): from ἀπό (*apo*) and στρέφω (*strepho*); ἀπό (*apo*) means away and implies distance; στρέφω (*strepho*) means to turn, to change, to switch positions; compounded, to turn away from, to change positions on an issue, to turn away from and to put distance between oneself and something else; to change one's allegiance; to reject
3. "ashamed" — ἐπαισχύνομαι (*epaischunomai*): disgraced; embarrassed; ashamed; red-faced with embarrassment; one embarrassed because he mistakenly believed a big lie; one embarrassed because he put his confidence in the wrong person or thing
4. "chain" — ἅλυσις (*halusis*): bond; physical chain; a manacle, handcuff, or chain
5. "sought" — ζητέω (*zeteo*): to seek, to search, or to look very intensively; a legal term to denote an intense investigation; denotes an intense and thorough searching, not a mere surface investigation; to search for thoroughly and exhaustively

6. "very diligently" — **σπουδάζω** (*spoudadzo*): to do something with eagerness; to do something with diligence; acting responsibly, quickly, and with attentiveness; one so diligent, excited and energetic, that he puts his whole heart into the principle or task before him

7. "found" — **εὑρίσκω** (*heurisko*): to find or to discover; a discovery made as a result of careful observance; a moment when one makes a surprising or conclusive discovery; usually points to a discovery made due to an intense investigation

8. "shortly" — **ταχύς** (*tachus*): to do something as swiftly as possible

9. "forsaken" — **ἐγκαταλείπω** (*egkataleipo*): here, to walk out on someone; to leave someone in a terrible condition; abandoning a person at the worst possible moment; to leave in the lurch; deserting a person in the most terrible way; it conveys the idea of abandonment

10. "present" — **νῦν** (*nun*): now, present, current

11. "world" — **αἰῶνος** (*aionos*): better translated age; depicts an age with a concrete beginning and a concrete ending; a measurable and limited age

12. "profitable" — **εὔχρηστος** (*euchrestos*): beneficial; profitable; well-adapted; useful

13. "cloak" — **φελόνης** (*phelones*): a traveling cloak, especially useful in foul weather

14. "books" — **βιβλίον** (*biblion*): here, plural; books

15. "especially" — **μάλιστα** (*malista*): especially; particularly; most of all in terms of importance

16. "parchments" — **μεμβράνα** (*membrana*): membranes; leather skins on which to write

17. "answer" — **ἀπολογία** (*apologia*): defense; trial in a court of law

18. "no man" — **οὐδείς** (*oudeis*): absolutely no one

19. "stood" — **παραγίνομαι** (*paristemi*): to step forward; to come alongside

20. "all" — **πάντες** (*pantes*): all, leaving no one out; all-inclusive

21. "forsook" — **ἐγκαταλείπω** (*egkataleipo*): here, to walk out on someone; to leave someone in a terrible condition; abandoning a person at the worst possible moment; to leave in the lurch; deserting a person in the most terrible way; the idea of abandonment

22. "by" — **δι'** (*di*): meaning through, indicating instrumentation

23. "delivered" — ῥύομαι (*ruomai*): to rescue, to deliver, to snatch, or even to drag out of danger; to save in the nick of time; a rescue operation intended to snatch a person out of physical or spiritual peril; intervention

SYNOPSIS

The emphasis of this lesson:

You have a choice in life: You can either remember all the people who have harmed you, or you can remember all the people God used to be a blessing to you. While Paul was in prison, hosts of people he previously poured his life into absolutely abandoned him, yet he made an important choice. Rather than focusing on those who abandoned him, he focused on how grateful he was for those who stuck with him faithfully until the end.

St. Isaac's Cathedral in Saint Petersburg, Russia, is simply magnificent. An amazing architect gave 40 years of his life to construct it, and then died one month after the building's consecration.

When people come into this cathedral, they see the marble, gold, and all its embellishments. A statue of the architect was placed in the cathedral so people would *never forget* the man who gave so much of his life to such a magnificent structure.

Likewise, there are people, places, and things in *your* life that you should *never forget*. When someone does something significant for you, never forget that person. When God displays His faithfulness and does something precious in your life, *never forget* it!

Your Memory Is a Powerful Tool If You Let It Work Positively for You

Psalm 103:1 and 2 says, "Bless the Lord, O my soul: and all that is within me, bless his holy name. Bless the Lord, O my soul, and forget not all his benefits." David was in a very low moment when he wrote this Psalm, and he was tempted to be depressed. Therefore, he knew he needed to speak to himself. He spoke to his soul — his mind, will, and emotions. He was saying, "Bless the Lord, *soul*! And don't forget all His benefits." Then David recalled the good things God did for him.

In the program, Rick shared, "One day, Denise and I were sitting together having a cup of coffee and tea and talking about our past. For some reason we began talking about all the people that had done wrong to us through the years. And the longer we talked, ugh…the room became darker, it became sullen, I felt myself sinking, and sinking, and sinking, and sinking."

"I said, 'Denise, what are we doing? Let's make a list of all the people that have been *good* to us.' I went and got a piece of paper and a pen, and we began to write down all the people that have been a blessing to us through the years, and it was pages and pages and pages! So many more people have been good to us than have been bad to us."

Don't Focus on People Who Turned on You, Instead, Remember People Who Were Good to You!

Timothy was in a very low moment because he felt like everyone had abandoned him. Paul encouraged him by saying, "This thou knowest, that all they which are in Asia be turned away from me; of whom are Phygellus and Hermogenes" (2 Timothy 1:15). Wait a minute! Paul's most successful ministry was in Asia!

It was in Asia that Paul worked in Assos, Colossae, Derbe, Didyma, Ephesus, Hierapolis, Iconium, Lystra, Antioch in Pisidia, Melitus, Perga, Troas, Smyrna, Pergamum, Sardis, Philadelphia, Laodicea, and many other cities. *Those are the places where Paul invested his life!* But when He was arrested and imprisoned in the city of Rome, suddenly, no one wanted to be close to him. People he had invested his life in and who he thought would always be faithful to him began bailing out on him.

Paul said, "…All they which are in Asia be turned away from me…" (2 Timothy 1:15). The Greek word *pantes,* translated here as "all," means *all; leaving no one out;* and *all-inclusive.* Paul was basically saying, "All they that be in Asia — all those churches I helped start, taught, and nurtured — they've *all* turned away from me." The Greek word *apostrepho* — translated as "be turned away" — comes from the word *apo* and *strepho.* The word *apo* means *away* and implies *distance;* and the word *strepho* pictures *to turn, to change,* or *to switch positions.* When compounded, this phrase "be turned away," translated from the Greek word *apostrepho,* means *to turn away from, to change positions on an issue, to turn away from and to put distance between oneself and something else;* or *to change one's allegiance.* It also means *to reject.*

In essence, Paul said, "Those who I thought would have allegiance to me for the rest of my life have suddenly changed their position concerning me. They've abandoned me; they've put space between themselves and me, and I've been rejected by them." Paul named two of them: Phygellus and Hermogenes. These two were well known Christian leaders who were with Paul in Rome, but then deserted him when he was arrested.

In The Midst of Difficulties, Choose To Remember Something Good

In spite of all the rejection from the people he poured so much into, Paul *decided* to focus on and remember someone who remained loyal to him. He said, "The Lord give mercy unto the house of Onesiphorus; for he oft refreshed me, and was not ashamed of my chain" (2 Timothy 1:16). While everyone else seemed to abandon him, one person was faithful, and Paul chose to remember *him*, and focus on him.

The word (and name) "Onesiphorus" is a Greek word which means *one who brings a benefit*. This man was a blessing and *a benefit* to Paul when he needed it. Paul said he "...was not ashamed of my chain." The word "ashamed" — the Greek word *epaischunomai* — describes one normally *disgraced; embarrassed; red-faced with embarrassment; one embarrassed because he mistakenly believed a big lie*. It pictures *one embarrassed because he put his confidence in the wrong person or thing*.

Onesiphorus didn't believe a big lie; he stuck with Paul and wasn't ashamed of his "chain." The word "chain" — the Greek word *halusis* — describes a *bond; physical chain; a manacle, handcuff, or chain*. Paul was imprisoned, and to be affiliated with him meant you also could be arrested and imprisoned. But Onesiphorus was such a faithful friend that Paul said, "But, when he was in Rome, he sought me out very diligently, and found me" (2 Timothy 1:17). How astounding! Because to seek Paul out meant Onesiphorus could have been imprisoned and even died for his faith. But he loved Paul so much he stuck with him.

Paul noted, "...He sought me out..." (2 Timothy 1:17). The Greek word *zeteo* — translated as "sought" — means *to seek, to search, or to look very intensively; an intense investigation*. It denotes *an intense and thorough searching, not a mere surface investigation*, and *to search for thoroughly and exhaustively*. Paul was imprisoned and so hidden away that Onesiphorus said, "I'm not going to stop until I find him." He searched and searched "very diligently," which is a translation of the Greek word *spoudadzo and* denotes *to do something with eagerness; to do something with diligence; acting responsibly, quickly, and with attentiveness.* It pictures *one so diligent, excited and energetic that he puts his whole heart into the principle or task before him.*

The Greek word *heurisko* — translated as "found" — means *to find or to discover; a discovery made as a result of careful observance; a moment when one makes a surprising or conclusive discovery;* and *usually points to a discovery made due to an intense investigation.* It's where we get the word "eureka!" It was a eureka moment when Onesiphorus found Paul after searching so diligently for him. "The Lord grant unto him that he may find mercy of the Lord in that day: and in how many things he ministered unto me at Ephesus, thou knowest very well" (2 Timothy 1:18).

Does Your Love for the Present World Exceed Your Love for God?

Paul continued, "Do thy diligence to come shortly unto me" (2 Timothy 4:9). The word "diligence" again, the Greek word *spoudadzo,* means *to do something with eagerness; to do something with diligence; acting responsibly, quickly, and with attentiveness.* It pictures *one so diligent, excited and energetic, that he puts his whole heart into the principle or task before him.* The word "shortly" — the Greek word *tachus* — means *to do something as swiftly as possible.* Why did Paul want Timothy to come to him as swiftly as possible? "For Demas hath forsaken me, having loved this present world, and is departed unto Thessalonica; Crescens to Galatia, Titus unto Dalmatia" (2 Timothy 4:10).

Demas was so notable in the Early Church that he was mentioned with Luke in scripture. Colossians 4:14 says, "Luke, the beloved physician, and Demas, greet you." But Demas abandoned Paul. In Second Timothy 4:10, Paul stated that Demas had "forsaken" him. The Greek word *egkataleipo* — translated as "forsaken" — pictures *to walk out on someone; to leave someone in a terrible condition; abandoning a person at the worst possible moment.* It denotes *to leave in the lurch* and *deserting a person in the most terrible way.* It conveys the idea of *abandonment.* It was the equivalent of saying, "He could not have chosen a worse moment to do what he did to me, and he did it because he loved this present world."

The word "love" is a word which normally describes our love for God. Demas had a choice: Either love the Lord or love the world. Paul noted that Demas chose to love this present world. The word "present" — the Greek word *nun* — depicts the *now, present*, or *current* world. The Greek word *aionos* — translated as "world" — is better translated as *age*. It depicts *an age with a concrete beginning and a concrete ending* and with *a measurable and limited age.*

Paul Purposely Thought on the People God Used To Be a Blessing to Him

Rather than focus on the abandonment and the desertion of Demas, Paul said, "Luke is right here." Second Timothy 4:11 declares, "Only Luke is with me...." How amazing! Luke, a physician, was Paul's faithful friend and traveling companion. This is the same Luke who wrote both the book of Luke and the book of Acts.

He was so committed that he went wherever Paul went, and if Paul was arrested, Luke — of his own accord — went to prison with him. There is no record that Luke was ever arrested, but when Paul was in prison, Luke was *with* him! He was faithful through every situation all the way to the end.

If You Made Mistakes in the Past, You Can Still Turn Things Around

In Second Timothy 4:11, Paul continues his instructions: "...Take Mark, and bring him with thee: for he is profitable to me for the ministry." The name "Mark" refers to John Mark, son of Mary and nephew of Barnabas, who traveled with Barnabas and Paul and was a source of conflict in their relationship. He later became an associate and scribe for Peter and penned the Gospel of Mark. Paul had a conflict with Barnabas over Mark in Acts 15, and the conflict was so terrible that it ruined the relationship between Paul and Barnabas. So Barnabas went one way, and Paul went another way.

It was a bad early experience with Mark, but now at the end of Paul's life, this young man who had so ruined his reputation totally *restored* it. Previously, Paul didn't want to do anything with Mark, but now he *needed* him. In fact, Paul said, "...He is profitable to me for the ministry" (2 Timothy 4:11). Mark ruined his testimony early in life, but years later, he's the very person Paul wanted to see.

"And Tychicus have I sent to Ephesus. The cloak that I left at Troas with Carpus, when thou comest, bring with thee, and the books, but especially the parchments" (2 Timothy 4:12,13). The Greek word *phelones* — translated as "cloak" — describes *a traveling cloak*, and one *especially useful in foul weather*. Winter was coming and the conditions in the prison were so terrible that Paul requested warmer clothes. Also, bring the "books" — the Greek word *biblion* — refers to *Old Testament* books. The Greek word *malista* — translated as "especially" — means *especially; particularly;* and *most of all in terms of importance.* These were parchments upon which Paul was going to write letters to the people he loved.

When Man Absolutely Abandons You, the Lord Will Stand With You

"At my first answer no man stood with me, but all men forsook me: I pray God that it may not be laid to their charge" (2 Timothy 4:16). The Greek word *apologia* — translated as "answer" — means *defense;* or his *trial in a court of law.* Paul basically said, "When I stood in court and was tried, no man stood with me." How sad that is. After all the people Paul stood with in life, when he needed them, undeniably "no man" stood with him. The words "no man" — the Greek word *oudeis* — means *absolutely no one.*

The Greek word *paristemi* — translated as "stood" — pictures *to step forward* or *to come alongside.* When Paul looked around the court room, they had all walked out, and he was there by himself. All men forsook him, but rather than focus on that, what did he say next? "Notwithstanding the Lord stood with me, and strengthened me; that by me the preaching might be fully known, and that all the Gentiles might hear: and I was delivered out of the mouth of the lion" (2 Timothy 4:17).

Remember How the Lord Stepped In!

Paul also declared that the Lord "stood" with him. Again, the word "stood" — the Greek word *paristemi* — means *to step forward* or *to come alongside.* Everybody disowned Paul; they all walked out on him. But that's when the Lord *stepped forward* on Paul's behalf. What happened when *God* stepped in? Second Timothy 4:17 says, "…He strengthened me; that by me…." The Greek word *di'* — translated as "by" — depicts *through* me, and indicates Paul became His *instrument.* Paul continued, "…That by me the preaching might be fully known, and that all the Gentiles might hear: and I was delivered out of the mouth of the lion" (2 Timothy 4:17).

The word "delivered" — the Greek word *ruomai* — means *to rescue, to deliver, to snatch,* or *to drag out of danger.* It denotes *to save in the nick of time,* and it pictures *a rescue operation intended to snatch a person out of physical or spiritual peril;* and *intervention.* The Lord came through for Paul!

Paul was sitting in prison probably thinking about his *own* future, but he ministered to Timothy who was afraid and hurt because people were unfaithful to him. He basically said, "Timothy, do you think you're going through something? All of Asia forsook me; people walked out on me. They couldn't have chosen a worse moment to do what they did. But I'm not going to focus on that! I choose to think about how Onesiphorus sought me out very diligently until he found me, and how *the Lord* stepped forward in my defense!"

Never forget the people who have been good to you, and how *God* has been good to you! He stepped forward in your defense in the past and He will do it again!

STUDY QUESTIONS

Study to shew thyself approved unto God, a workman that needeth not to be ashamed, rightly dividing the word of truth.
— 2 Timothy 2:15

1. What are seven benefits Psalm 103:1-6 admonishes you to *remember*?
2. Read Mark 2:1-12 and see the importance of not only *having* faith-filled friends, but also *being* a faith-filled friend! Four friends helped a man who was sick of the palsy by uncovering the roof and getting him to Jesus so he could be healed. What are you willing to do to help someone in need? (*Consider* Luke 10:25-37.)
3. In Second Timothy 4:10, Paul stated that Demas had forsaken him, "having loved this present world." First John 2:15 says, "Love not the world, neither the things that are in the world. If any man love the world, the love of the Father is not in him." Also read Second Timothy 3:1-5. How can you keep your love for God ablaze, and resist the lure of the age we live in?

PRACTICAL APPLICATION

But be ye doers of the word, and not hearers only, deceiving your own selves.
— James 1:22

1. *People* have been good to you. Rather than remembering all those who have hurt you, take out a piece of paper or a journal and make a list of all the people who have been *good* to you! Purposely remember the loyal people God placed in your life who have been kind to you, led you to Christ, prayed for you, and more. In fact, pick up the phone and call them and thank them for what they've done for you.

2. *God* has been good to you. Write down all the big (and little) things He has done for you and your family and take time to sincerely praise and thank Him for them. You'll find strength as you remember the many ways He displayed His goodness toward you.

3. Paul was abandoned by many people he had poured his life into, yet a few faithful friends stuck with him, and *the Lord* stood with him! Have you ever felt abandoned? Maybe you've experienced the sting of betrayal from a loved one or close friend. Rather than sink in the pain of rejection, rise up and focus on the truth: God *loves* you, He is *for* you, *with* you, *in* you, and *on your side.* Man may have separated himself from you, but there is One who will never separate Himself from you! Saturate yourself with the truth that He is *with* you by meditating on the following verses.

   • "...For He [God] Himself has said, I will not in any way fail you *nor* give you up *nor* leave you without support. [I will] not, [I will] not, [I will] not in any degree leave you helpless *nor* forsake *nor* let [you] down (relax My hold on you)! [Assuredly not!]" (Hebrews 13:5 *AMPC*).

   • "Have I not commanded you? Be strong and courageous. Do not be frightened, and do not be dismayed, for the Lord your God is with you wherever you go" (Joshua 1:9 *ESV*).

   • "For I am sure that neither death nor life, nor angels nor rulers, nor things present nor things to come, nor powers, nor height nor depth, nor anything else in all creation, will be able to separate us from the love of God in Christ Jesus our Lord" (Romans 8:38,39 *ESV*).

Notes

_____

_____

_____

_____

_____

_____

_____

_____

_____

_____

_____

_____

_____

_____

_____

_____

_____

_____

_____

_____

_____

_____

_____

_____

_____

_____

_____

_____

Notes

www.ingramcontent.com/pod-product-compliance
Lightning Source LLC
Chambersburg PA
CBHW051047030426
42339CB00006B/240